A Note From Rick Renner

I am on a personal quest to see a "revival of the Bible" so people can establish their lives on a firm foundation that will stand strong and endure the test as end-time storm winds begin to intensify.

In order to experience a revival of the Bible in your personal life, it is important to take time each day to read, receive, and apply its truths to your life. James tells us that if we will continue in the perfect law of liberty — refusing to be forgetful hearers, but determined to be doers — we will be blessed in our ways. As you watch or listen to the programs in this series and work through this corresponding study guide, I trust you will search the Scriptures and allow the Holy Spirit to help you hear something new from God's Word that applies specifically to your life. I encourage you to be a doer of the Word He reveals to you. Whatever the cost, I assure you — it will be worth it.

> Thy words were found, and I did eat them;
> and thy word was unto me the joy and rejoicing of mine heart:
> for I am called by thy name, O Lord God of hosts.
> — Jeremiah 15:16

Your brother and friend in Jesus Christ,

Rick Renner

God Has Given You the Victory

Copyright © 2019 by Rick Renner
1814 W. Tacoma St.
Broken Arrow, OK 74012-1406

Published by Rick Renner Ministries
www.renner.org

ISBN: 978-1-6803-1603-2

ISBN 13 eBook: 978-1-6803-1641-4

How To Use This Study Guide

This five-lesson study guide corresponds to *God Has Given You the Victory With Rick Renner* (Renner TV). Each lesson in this study guide covers a topic that is addressed during the program series, with questions and references supplied to draw you deeper into your own private study of the Scriptures on this subject.

To derive the most benefit from this study guide, consider the following:

First, watch or listen to the program prior to working through the corresponding lesson in this guide. (Programs can also be viewed at **renner.org** by clicking on the Media/Archives links or on our Renner Ministries YouTube channel.)

Second, take the time to look up the scriptures included in each lesson. Prayerfully consider their application to your own life.

Third, use a journal or notebook to make note of your answers to each lesson's Study Questions and Practical Application challenges.

Fourth, invest specific time in prayer and in the Word of God to consult with the Holy Spirit. Write down the scriptures or insights He reveals to you.

Finally, take action! Whatever the Lord tells you to do according to His Word, do it.

For added insights on this subject, it is recommended that you obtain Rick Renner's book *The Will of God: The Key to Your Success* . You may also select from Rick's other available resources by placing your order at **renner.org** or by calling 1-800-742-5593.

TOPIC

Victory Will Be Yours if You Follow God's Instructions

SCRIPTURES

1. **Joshua 6:1-13** — Now Jericho was straitly shut up because of the children of Israel: none went out, and none came in. And the Lord said unto Joshua, See, I have given into thine hand Jericho, and the king thereof, and the mighty men of valour. And ye shall compass the city, all ye men of war, and go round about the city once. Thus shalt thou do six days. And seven priests shall bear before the ark seven trumpets of rams' horns: and the seventh day ye shall compass the city seven times, and the priests shall blow with the trumpets. And it shall come to pass, that when they make a long blast with the ram's horn, and when ye hear the sound of the trumpet, all the people shall shout with a great shout; and the wall of the city shall fall down flat, and the people shall ascend up every man straight before him. And Joshua the son of Nun called the priests, and said unto them, Take up the ark of the covenant, and let seven priests bear seven trumpets of rams' horns before the ark of the Lord. And he said unto the people, Pass on, and compass the city, and let him that is armed pass on before the ark of the Lord. And it came to pass, when Joshua had spoken unto the people, that the seven priests bearing the seven trumpets of rams' horns passed on before the Lord, and blew with the trumpets: and the ark of the covenant of the Lord followed them. And the armed men went before the priests that blew with the trumpets, and the rereward came after the ark, the priests going on, and blowing with the trumpets. And Joshua had commanded the people, saying, Ye shall not shout, nor make any noise with your voice, neither shall any word proceed out of your mouth, until the day I bid you shout; then shall ye shout. So the ark of the Lord compassed the city, going about it once: and they came into the camp, and lodged in the camp. And Joshua rose early in the morning, and the priests took up the ark of the Lord. And seven priests bearing seven trumpets of rams' horns before the ark of the Lord went on continually, and blew

with the trumpets: and the armed men went before them; but the rereward came after the ark of the Lord, the priests going on, and blowing with the trumpets. Joshua rose early in the morning, and the priests took up the ark of the Lord. And seven priests bearing seven trumpets of rams' horns before the ark of the Lord went on continually, and blew with the trumpets: and the armed men went before them; but the rereward came after the ark of the Lord, the priests going on, and blowing with the trumpets. And the second day they compassed the city once, and returned into the camp: so they did six days. And it came to pass on the seventh day, that they rose early about the dawning of the day, and compassed the city after the same manner seven times: only on that day they compassed the city seven times. And it came to pass at the seventh time, when the priests blew with the trumpets, Joshua said unto the people, Shout; for the Lord hath given you the city.

SYNOPSIS

The five lessons in this study entitled *God Has Given You the Victory* will focus on the following topics:

- Victory Will Be Yours if You Follow God's Instructions
- Do What You Know To Do To Get Your Victory
- The Consequences of Disobedience
- Getting Back on Track to Victory
- The Fruit of Obedience

The emphasis of this lesson:

God promised Joshua and the people of Israel victory over the city of Jericho, but it would only be achieved by His power through obedience to His instructions.

One of the most important cities of the Jordan Valley was the ancient city of Jericho. It is identified as the oldest city in the world, and it is first mentioned in the Bible in Numbers 22 as the place where the Israelites camped as they were conquering the cities east of the Jordan River. Jericho would be the first city in the Promised Land that Joshua would lead Israel to conquer — it was to be a firstfruits offering to the Lord. Although God had promised certain victory, it would only be obtained under one condition: Joshua and his people were to explicitly follow God's instructions, which is exactly what they did.

All of us want and need victory in our lives, and through faith in Jesus Christ, victory is our inheritance. Whether it's victory over fear and anxiety, financial lack, sickness and disease, or challenges in our relationships, we are destined to win in every situation we face as long as we will listen to the Lord and obey His instructions explicitly.

Victory Requires Actions of Faith

Our story opens in Joshua 6. The children of Israel have just crossed the divinely parted waters of the Jordan River, and they were preparing to take their first city in the Promised Land. The Bible says, "Now Jericho was straitly shut up because of the children of Israel: none went out, and none came in. And the Lord said unto Joshua, See, I have given into thine hand Jericho, and the king thereof, and the mighty men of valour" (vv. 1,2).

Naturally speaking, Jericho and its people were safe within their walls. The city was under lockdown, and the idea that *Israel had already conquered them* was a ridiculous notion in their minds. Nevertheless, God had told Joshua, "It's yours — the city of Jericho, its mighty warriors, and its king have all been given to you." This monumental defeat of an otherwise impenetrable city was *a finished work* and *a done deed* in the mind of God. But in order to carry it out and take possession, there was a specific plan of action Israel needed to carry out.

This was essentially what God told Joshua when he had just become the leader of the nation. The Lord said, "Moses my servant is dead; now therefore arise, go over this Jordan, thou, and all this people, unto the land which I do give to them, even to the children of Israel" (Joshua 1:2). The land was promised by God to Israel, but in order for them to claim it, they needed to physically walk through it. God said, "Every place that the sole of your foot shall tread upon, that have I given unto you…" (Joshua 1:3).

The people of Israel were to take possession of the land *step-by-step* by faith. God required them to put their faith in action in order for the territory of promise to rightfully become theirs. The same is true for you. God will give you a promised dream or vision of how He wants to bless your life, but in order for it to become reality, there are certain steps you will have to walk out in faith.

God Gave *Specific* Instructions

In Joshua 6:3 and 4, the Lord began to unveil His blueprint for victory over the city of Jericho. He said, "And ye shall compass the city, all ye men of war, and go round about the city once. Thus shalt thou do six days. And seven priests shall bear before the ark seven trumpets of rams' horns: and the seventh day ye shall compass the city seven times, and the priests shall blow with the trumpets."

God said that all the "men of war," which were all the men of Israel who were 20 years old or older, were to walk around, or encompass, the city once a day for six days. Then on the seventh day, they were to march around the city seven times, and when they were done, the priests were to blow their "trumpets," which refers to rams' horns or shofars.

God's directions were simple and clear. Although they may have been difficult to understand and seemed unorthodox, the people were to fully obey those instructions. Lack of action or a refusal to obey for any reason would result in *no victory*. Victory over Jericho would only be experienced through faith. God was setting a standard by which all the other cities in Canaan would be taken.

Likewise, you may not always understand why God tells you to do certain things, but He is always right, regardless. Whatever He tells you to do, obey it explicitly, and you'll reap the reward of victory — just as Joshua and the children of Israel did.

The Purpose for Sounding a Ram's Horn

According to Joshua 6:4, seven priests each carrying a shofar were to walk before the Ark of the Covenant and sound their horn just after their seventh trip around the wall on the seventh day. Israel regularly used rams' horns, especially on four specific occasions:

- Whenever they were going make a sacrifice of faith.
- To declare in faith that the presence of God was with them as they marched forward.
- Just before their men of war entered into battle. At Jericho, it was spiritual warfare in the realest sense, as the Israelites were doing something that could only be accomplished by the power of God's Spirit going with them and performing His part.

- Whenever Israel experienced great victory. The blowing of the ram's horn was a declaration of celebration. And in the case of Jericho, the sounding of rams' horns on the seventh day was a declaration that victory was theirs.

The Reason for the Shout

In addition to telling them to blow the rams' horns, God instructed the people of Israel *to give a great shout.* Joshua 6:5 says, "And it shall come to pass, that when they make a long blast with the ram's horn, and when ye hear the sound of the trumpet, all the people shall shout with a great shout; and the wall of the city shall fall down flat, and the people shall ascend up every man straight before him."

The people of Israel would lift up a great shout:

- To initiate or announce the start of each battle.
- As an expression of faith.
- To express great joy.
- To put the enemy to flight.

Interestingly, in each of these situations, *faith* was required in order to shout. In other words, the people of Israel probably didn't *feel* like shouting when the walls of Jericho were standing strong right in front of them.

Likewise, we don't always feel like giving a great shout when our problems tower over us and seem impenetrable. A shout of victory requires *faith.*

Joshua Received God's Directives and Mobilized the People To Move Forward

When Joshua called the priests to take up the Ark of the Covenant — and positioned the seven priests with their shofars in front of the ark — he said to the people, "...Pass on, and compass the city, and let him that is armed pass on before the ark of the Lord" (Joshua 6:7).

First, notice that Joshua said, "Pass on." This was Joshua's directive *to proceed.* Even though the Israelites had no visual proof that the wall was about to fall, they had been commanded by God to begin marching around the city, and it was time to get up and get moving.

Next, Joshua said, "Compass the city." The word "compass" means *to move forward in an organized fashion with determination*. Israel was to put all their energy into what God had told them to do — and to do it to the best of their ability.

Also notice what they were to compass — "the city." God didn't just say, "Randomly begin marching." He gave them a target, a goal, an objective. They were to harness all their energy, efforts, and focus on accomplishing a specific objective: to march around the city of Jericho to see it conquered.

Last, Joshua said, "Let him that is armed pass on before the ark of the Lord." In other words, it's time to begin making forward movement. This is the same thing God is saying to you. It is time to quit sitting around wishing for things to change. It's time for you to "pass on." In faith, God wants you to get on your feet and with your "trumpet" in hand, begin moving forward in what He has told you to do. Start shouting that the victory is yours, in Jesus' name.

God Told Israel When To Shout and When To Be Silent

Joshua 6:8-10 says, "And it came to pass, when Joshua had spoken unto the people, that the seven priests bearing the seven trumpets of rams' horns passed on before the Lord, and blew with the trumpets: and the ark of the covenant of the Lord followed them. And the armed men went before the priests that blew with the trumpets, and the rereward came after the ark, the priests going on, and blowing with the trumpets. And Joshua had commanded the people, saying, Ye shall not shout, nor make any noise with your voice, neither shall any word proceed out of your mouth, until the day I bid you shout; then shall ye shout."

For six days, the people were to march around the city and not utter a word. It is very likely that if the people were to have begun talking, they would have talked themselves out of their victory. Given the track record of their family lineage, they would have likely said things such as, "What in the world are we doing? This just doesn't make any sense. What is going to become of us? There is no guarantee that this is going to work. This is so foolish."

Fear, doubt, unbelief, negativity, cynicism, etc. are often what our mouth defaults to when we don't understand what God is doing. In fact, if we're not careful, we can quickly talk ourselves right out of obedience. God knew that, which is why He told the people of Israel, through Joshua, to be quiet and not utter a sound until the seventh day when they were to give a great shout.

Israel Stayed True to God's Plan

The instructions had been given and the people took their positions. All that was left to do was to obediently walk out God's plan. "So the ark of the Lord compassed the city, going about it once: and they came into the camp, and lodged in the camp" (Joshua 6:11). As soon as the Israelites were finished on their first day, they returned to their headquarters to regroup and recharge. At their camp, they could strengthen and encourage each other, pray together, hear God's word of instruction, and rest before beginning the next day.

In the same way, you need a "camp" in which you can lodge. This would include a church that you call home and a small group of people with which you can share friendship and life. People with whom you share the same beliefs, goals, and challenges are a great encouragement and strength to you. They can help you stick with God's plan and stay on track until you see victory.

Verses 12-14 go on to say, "Joshua rose early in the morning, and the priests took up the ark of the Lord. And seven priests bearing seven trumpets of rams' horns before the ark of the Lord went on continually, and blew with the trumpets: and the armed men went before them; but the rereward came after the ark of the Lord, the priests going on, and blowing with the trumpets. And the second day they compassed the city once, and returned into the camp: so they did six days."

On days one, two, three, four, five, and six, they obeyed God's word explicitly. Was it monotonous? Did it require discipline and determination? Yes, but it led to their victory.

Don't Become Bored With Your Obedience

Israel faithfully carried out what God had commanded them to do, and it resulted in victory. Joshua 6:15 and 16 says, "And it came to pass on the seventh day, that they rose early about the dawning of the day, and compassed the city after the same manner seven times: only on that day they compassed the city seven times. And it came to pass at the seventh time, when the priests blew with the trumpets, Joshua said unto the people, Shout; for the Lord hath given you the city."

For six days they had done the same thing over and over again, and nothing in the natural was changed. The walls of the city were still standing, and the people of Jericho were safe inside. More than likely, the people of Israel were tempted to think, *Is there any sense at all to what we're doing?* Nevertheless, on the seventh day when Joshua gave the signal for everyone to shout and they obeyed, the mighty walls of Jericho came tumbling down!

Friend, if you want to taste the sweet victory God has promised, stick to the plan He gave you. Even if progress is slow or nothing seems to be changing, or the task you've undertaken is monotonous, *never give up!* There is light at the end of your tunnel. The finish line is just ahead, and you are about to break the winner's ribbon! Be faithful to the end and you will win!

STUDY QUESTIONS

Study to shew thyself approved unto God, a workman that needeth not to be ashamed, rightly dividing the word of truth.
— 2 Timothy 2:15

1. God declared victory over Jericho for Joshua and the people of Israel *before* they had taken any action. This reveals a major aspect of God's character, which we see in Isaiah 46:9 and 10 (also *consider* Isaiah 42:9; Daniel 2:28; and Matthew 24:36). How does this aspect of His character motivate you to seek and obey Him more?
2. According to Psalm 34:12,13, Proverbs 13:3, and Proverbs 21:23, what are the rewards of guarding and controlling your tongue?
3. Have you become bored with your obedience? In what ways does God's promise in Galatians 6:9 encourage you to keep on keeping on? (Also *consider* Proverbs 24:16; 1 Corinthians 15:57,58.)

PRACTICAL APPLICATION

But be ye doers of the word, and not hearers only, deceiving your own selves.
— James 1:22

1. Just as the people of Israel had a camp where they could rest and recharge, you need one too. Your local church serves in this way. What place of weekly fellowship do you call home? What aspects about it encourage and strengthen you most?

2. Have you ever talked yourself out of victory? Do you need help keeping your mouth shut in that regard? If so, read Psalm 141:3 and turn it into a personal prayer to God.

LESSON 2

TOPIC

Do What You Know To Do To Get Your Victory

SCRIPTURES

1. **Joshua 1:2,3** — Moses my servant is dead; now therefore arise, go over this Jordan, thou, and all this people, unto the land which I do give to them, even to the children of Israel. Every place that the sole of your foot shall tread upon, that have I given unto you....

2. **Joshua 6:16-21** — And it came to pass at the seventh time, when the priests blew with the trumpets, Joshua said unto the people, Shout; for the Lord hath given you the city. And the city shall be accursed, even it, and all that are therein... And ye, in any wise keep yourselves from the accursed thing, lest ye make yourselves accursed, when ye take of the accursed thing, and make the camp of Israel a curse, and trouble it. But all the silver, and gold, and vessels of brass and iron, are consecrated unto the Lord: they shall come into the treasury of the Lord. So the people shouted when the priests blew with the trumpets: and it came to pass, when the people heard the sound of the trumpet, and the people shouted with a great shout, that the wall fell down flat, so that the people went up into the city, every man straight before him, and they took the city. And they utterly destroyed all that was in the city, both man and woman, young and old, and ox, and sheep, and ass, with the edge of the sword.

3. **Joshua 6:27** — So the Lord was with Joshua; and his fame was noised throughout all the country.

SYNOPSIS

Jericho, also known as the city of palm trees, was in existence thousands of years before Joshua was born. In some places, its walls stood more than 20 feet high and were nearly 20 feet thick. Indeed, Jericho's mammoth structure and longevity were symbols of military might and invincibility. Yet God told Joshua that the city, its king, and its mighty men had all been given into his hand — *if* he and Israel would explicitly follow God's directions.

The instructions were simple: For six days, all the men of Israel, aged 20 and above, were to march one time around the city in silence. The Ark of the Covenant was to go before them, and seven priests with rams' horns were to lead the way. On the seventh and last day, Israel was to march around the city seven times, and once the seventh lap was completed, the priests were to give a loud blast on their shofars. The people were then to give a great shout, and the victory over Jericho would be sealed.

The emphasis of this lesson:

Just as Joshua and the children of Israel obtained victory over Jericho, you can defeat any enemy that stands before you if you will listen to the Word of God and obey His Holy Spirit.

The Israelites Were 'Professional Walkers'

After living a full life of 120 years, Moses breathed his last breath and was buried in the land of Moab, east of the Jordan River. Joshua the son of Nun took his place as Israel's leader, and the Lord spoke to him saying, "Moses my servant is dead; now therefore arise, go over this Jordan, thou, and all this people, unto the land which I do give to them, even to the children of Israel" (Joshua 1:2).

What a wonderful promise. The land of Canaan, located on the west side of the Jordan was given by God to the people of Israel. This was certainly reason to celebrate and shout praises to God. But then the Lord added a qualifying condition to His promise. He said, "Every place *that the sole of your foot shall tread upon*, that have I given unto you..." (v. 3). This meant that in order to take possession of the land, the Israelites would physically have to "walk it out," one step at a time.

With every step the children of Israel took, they gained more territory. Day after day, as they obediently followed the Lord's instructions, more and more of the Promised Land became theirs. If there was anything the people of Israel knew how to do, it was how to walk! Considering all the traveling afoot that they did for 40 years in the wilderness, some might have even called them *professional walkers*.

If you think about it, the fact that God didn't give the Israelites *all* of the Promised Land *all* at once was a huge blessing. They really weren't familiar with the land, so they couldn't have managed it properly. They also didn't know what challenges awaited them or where they would run into those challenges. Therefore, as they traveled the land one step at a time, they learned more and more about the territory God had promised them. Then they took control over it little by little *by faith*.

Do What You Know to Do — *Use* What You Know to Use

It's interesting to note that God didn't tell the Israelites to do something they had no experience doing. He told them to do what they knew to do — to use their feet. Wherever Israel walked, God worked supernaturally.

You will find that when God gives you instructions, they are usually very simple. He will usually tell you to do things you already know how to do. Take Moses for example. He knew how to use a shepherd's staff, as he had used one for about 40 years. Then there was David. When he faced the giant Goliath, God prompted him to use the sling he had used countless times previously, and he was victorious.

How about you? What's your God-given dream or vision? Is it singing? Is it writing? In the simplest of terms, what victory are you trying to attain? You don't have to be a theologian or Bible scholar to accomplish what He has placed in your heart. Just use what you know how to use — employ your hands, your feet, your voice, and your talents.

In other words, don't try to go so spiritually deep that you miss the practical, simple ways God works. Whatever the Lord has given you, use it every day and at every opportunity He provides to fulfill His calling on your life. Every place the sole of your foot lands will become new territory for you to take and manage for His glory. Little by little, you will achieve your goal. That is how God works with us.

Blow the Trumpets and Give a Great Shout!

As we learned in the first lesson, after the Israelites completed their seventh time around Jericho, the priests leading the way were to blow their trumpets, and the people were to shout; for the Lord had given them the city (*see* Joshua 6:16).

Trumpets, also known as rams' horns or shofars, were sounded for *four primary reasons*. First, they were blown *to announce a time of great sacrifice*. Second, they were sounded *to declare that the presence of the Lord was with Israel*. Third, they were blown *to signify a battle was beginning*. And lastly, shofars were sounded *to declare that victory had been won*.

Shouts were also primarily sounded on *four occasions*. The first was *to declare that a battle was commencing*; it was the last action before a battle began. Second, a shout was made *as an expression of faith*. Third, the people of Israel shouted *to express joy* — it was a joyful shout of victory. And the fourth occasion for giving a great shout was *to instill fear into the hearts of their enemies and put them to flight*.

In the taking of Jericho, God instructed Israel to *blow trumpets* and *give a great shout*. In other words, they were to utilize all their efforts. In doing so, they were declaring that: 1) their march forward was a sacrifice of faith; 2) the presence of God was with them; 3) they were entering into battle; and 4) by faith, they had victory over Jericho.

In all their efforts, faith was required. In the natural, nothing had changed. The walls of the city were still standing, and there was no visual evidence that anything miraculous was taking place. Essentially, God was telling Israel (and He is also telling us), "Don't be moved by what you see; be obedient to what I said, and victory will follow. Blow the trumpets and shout as loud as you can, for I, the Lord, have given you the city."

Jericho Was the Firstfruits of the Promised Land

In all of God's instructions, there was a word of warning. Joshua 6:17-19 says, "And the city shall be accursed, even it, and all that are therein.... And ye, in any wise keep yourselves from the accursed thing, lest ye make yourselves accursed, when ye take of the accursed thing, and make the camp of Israel a curse, and trouble it. But all the silver, and gold, and vessels of brass and iron, are consecrated unto the Lord: they shall come into the treasury of the Lord."

These verses tell us that Jericho and everything in it were dedicated and set apart for God and God alone. It represents the *firstfruits* of all that God was about to give to Israel. In faith, they were to bring all the silver, gold, and vessels of brass and iron into the treasury of the Lord. For them to take any of these "accursed" things for themselves would make them accursed.

This idea of a curse is mentioned four times in verse 18, so it is extremely important to understand. The "accursed thing" is anything you take that belongs to the Lord. If the people of Israel disobeyed and took anything that was "accursed," they would bring a curse on themselves and cause trouble for all of Israel. Again, Jericho was the first city they were taking possession of in the new land — it was the firstfruits of all the land the Lord was giving them, and it was "consecrated unto the Lord" (*see* Joshua 6:19). To take something from Jericho was to take what belonged to God.

As you study further in Scripture, you will see that the Lord told Israel to plunder and take for themselves from all the other cities they conquered. However, Jericho was the firstfruits, and it belonged to the Lord.

Israel's Obedience Brought Supernatural Results

Israel faithfully obeyed the instruction of the Lord, marching around the city one time for six days and seven times on the seventh day. Then, as directed, the people shouted when the priests blew with the trumpets. "... And it came to pass, when the people heard the sound of the trumpet, and the people shouted with a great shout, that the wall fell down flat, so that the people went up into the city, every man straight before him, and they took the city. And they utterly destroyed all that was in the city, both man and woman, young and old, and ox, and sheep, and ass, with the edge of the sword" (Joshua 6:20,21).

Joshua and the people of Israel carried out the plan of the Lord and wiped out everything and everyone in Jericho — everyone except Rahab and all who were in her house with her. She had protected the lives of the two Israeli spies who came to survey the land. Therefore the Lord spared the lives of her and her household. In fact, Rahab's devotion to God touched

Him so greatly that He engrafted her into the genealogy of Jesus Christ (*see* Matthew 1:1-16).

Did all of God's instructions make sense to the people of Israel? Probably not, which is important for us to realize. Many times the Holy Spirit will tell us to do things that seem foolish, fruitless, or unnecessary. Nevertheless, if we will obey His directions and stick with His plan explicitly, we will see victory just as Israel did.

When Jesus told His disciples that they were going to feed 5,000 men and their families with five loaves and two fish, it made no sense to their natural minds. Yet by faith, they obeyed Jesus, directing the people to sit and prepare to receive the meal that was on its way. As they closed their mouths to doubt, unbelief, and negativity — and opened their hearts to the supernatural power of Jesus — they witnessed the greatest miracle of multiplication and food distribution ever seen (*see* Matthew 14:15-21).

Friend, God has a personal plan to bring you into victory. If you will seek the Lord and listen to Him, He will give you directions. As you obey Him, supernatural results will be yours! It doesn't matter how tough or fierce the enemy is that is standing in front of you. He will fall flat on his face just as the walls of Jericho fell flat to the ground — if you will choose to explicitly obey what the Lord has instructed you to do.

STUDY QUESTIONS

Study to shew thyself approved unto God, a workman that needeth not to be ashamed, rightly dividing the word of truth.
— 2 Timothy 2:15

1. God didn't give the Israelites *all* of the Promised Land *all* at once. Instead, He gave it to them *little by little*. Carefully read Exodus 23:27-30, which confirms this fact and tells why the Lord chose to do things this way. What does this say to you personally about the enemies you face in your life?

2. Jericho was the "firstfruits" of the Promised Land. Proverbs 3:9 and 10 says, "Honour the Lord with thy substance, and with the *firstfruits* of all thine increase: so shall thy barns be filled with plenty, and thy presses shall burst out with new wine." What do you think "barns" represent in your life? How about "wine vats" that will burst out with "new wine"?

PRACTICAL APPLICATION

**But be ye doers of the word, and not hearers only,
deceiving your own selves.
— James 1:22**

1. For Joshua and the people of Israel, Jericho was an enemy that they were called to conquer. What enemy (or problem) is directly in front of you that you know you need to defeat?

2. What specific instructions has God given you thus far to bring about the victory He has promised? Describe it briefly.

3. Are you obediently walking out what God has instructed you to do? In not, why?

4. If there's something God has told you to do that you are struggling to obey, how is this lesson helping you to obey His instructions?

LESSON 3

TOPIC

The Consequences of Disobedience

SCRIPTURES

1. **Joshua 6:20,21** — So the people shouted when the priests blew with the trumpets: and it came to pass, when the people heard the sound of the trumpet, and the people shouted with a great shout, that the wall fell down flat, so that the people went up into the city, every man straight before him, and they took the city.

2. **Joshua 7:1** — But the children of Israel committed a trespass in the accursed thing: for Achan, the son of Carmi, the son of Zabdi, the son of Zerah, of the tribe of Judah, took of the accursed thing: and the anger of the Lord was kindled against the children of Israel.

SYNOPSIS

The ancient city of Jericho has undergone many excavations, revealing evidence of a people who lived thousands of years ago in a citadel that was extremely fortified. Soldiers positioned on top of its walls could see enemies approaching from many miles away and deal with them quickly. To defeat the people of Jericho would take an act of God, which is exactly what happened.

As Joshua and the people of Israel perfectly obeyed the Lord's directions, the Lord perfectly did what He promised. After marching around Jericho in faith for seven days, the people gave a great shout when the priests blew their trumpets. The walls of the city supernaturally fell to the ground, and Israel went into the city and laid it waste (*see* Joshua 6:20,21). Yet, after Jericho was wiped out, the Bible says, "the children of Israel committed a trespass…" (Joshua 7:1). What was this "trespass," and what effect did it have on God's people?

The emphasis of this lesson:

Just as obedience to God's directions brings blessings, disobedience yields unwanted consequences. Achan's trespass did this very thing to Israel just after their triumph over Jericho.

God's Warning to Israel

Before the people of Israel went into the city of Jericho, God gave them a clear and sober warning: "And the city shall be accursed, even it, and all that are therein… And ye, in any wise keep yourselves from the accursed thing, lest ye make yourselves accursed, when ye take of the accursed thing, and make the camp of Israel a curse, and trouble it" (Joshua 6:17,18).

We saw in our last lesson that the "accursed thing" in this context was anything that belonged to God. Jericho was the first city in the new land to be taken by Israel. Thus it was the *firstfruits* of all the land and possessions that God was about to give them. He explicitly told Israel that "… all the silver, and gold, and vessels of brass and iron, are consecrated unto the Lord: they shall come into the treasury of the Lord" (Joshua 6:19). To take something from Jericho was to take from the Lord Himself, which is exactly what someone did.

Joshua 7:1 says, "But the children of Israel committed a trespass in the accursed thing: for Achan, the son of Carmi, the son of Zabdi, the son of Zerah, of the tribe of Judah, took of the accursed thing: and the anger of the Lord was kindled against the children of Israel." Interestingly, it wasn't all of Israel that disobeyed the Lord. It was *just one man* — Achan.

Yet God held the entire nation responsible, which shows the far-reaching effects of one man's sin.

Sin and disobedience is never a minor thing. It can have major repercussions on an individual, on his family, on his church, or even on a nation. Remember, sin and death and the empowerment of Satan in the affairs of men entered the whole human race through Adam's *one act* of disobedience. But also remember that through Jesus' obedience, we are experiencing all the blessings of being made right with God!

What Is a Trespass?

Achan's act of disobedience was called a "trespass." Unlike a normal sin, which is missing the mark of God's standard, a "trespass" is *a knowledgeable act of wrong*. It is *knowingly violating a rule or another person's rights or possessions*. Many times we sin and don't even realize we've done it. This is a manifestation of the sin nature. A trespass, on the other hand, is *a deliberate violation*; there is nothing accidental about it.

There are a number of examples of trespasses in the Bible. For instance, *adultery* is a trespass. It is not an accidental mistake or a simple sin. Adultery is done with knowledge that you are violating someone's spouse.

Stealing is a trespass. It is not a mistake or a simple sin; it is done knowing that you are violating another person's possessions.

Murmuring and complaining is a trespass, not a mistake. God has clearly stated in His Word that He is against it — in fact, He hates it. It is what caused Him to bring punishment on the children of Israel after they came out of Egypt (*see* Numbers 14). If you murmur and complain, you do it with full knowledge that God is against it.

Lying is a trespass; it is not a mistake. It bothers your conscience and takes away your peace. When you lie, you do it knowing that you're crossing the line of what is right and wrong.

Gossiping is a trespass, not a mistake. When you gossip, you're going where you haven't been invited. It is knowingly engaging in conversation about someone else's business that could scar his or her reputation.

Not tithing is a trespass, not a mistake. If you know what the Bible says about tithing, and you don't tithe, you know you are not giving God what is rightfully His; you're using it for other purposes, and it brings a curse.

Any activity that you know is wrong, but you engage in it, anyway, is a trespass. All of us have been guilty of trespasses. That is why Jesus taught us to pray that God would forgive us our trespasses as we forgive others who trespass against us (*see* Matthew 6:12). We are actually asking Him to forgive our own violations as we forgive those who have violated us.

Achan committed a trespass. He and all of Israel had been warned by the Lord not to take anything from Jericho because it was consecrated to the Lord. He knew that he was violating God's instructions, and it was a serious trespass in the Lord's sight. His single act of disobedience opened the door for defeat to come to all of Israel.

Thirteen Things That Kindle the Anger of the Lord

According to Joshua 7:1, Achan's trespass of taking of the accursed thing *kindled the anger of the Lord* against Israel. A careful study of Scripture reveals that there are certain things that kindle the Lord's anger. Here are 13 specific things.

Stubbornness kindles God's anger. When Moses argued with God about being sent to Pharaoh, it infuriated the Lord (*see* Exodus 4:10-14). When God's people are obstinate and argue with Him about what He wants them to do, it angers Him.

Idolatry angers God. When God's people give their devotion to things other than Him, it angers the Lord (*see* Exodus 32:19-22; Numbers 25:3; Deuteronomy 9:20).

Murmuring kindles the Lord's anger. When the children of Israel complained and murmured against Moses, God's anointed leader, it angered the Lord (*see* Numbers 11:1,10). Be careful what you say about your pastor, your president, and your leaders. God sees and hears everything.

Ingratitude angers God. When God has been good to people and they are not thankful, but instead gripe and complain about everything, it angers the Lord greatly.

Insubordination ignites the anger of God. Remember when Miriam and Aaron spoke against Moses and claimed that they were just as anointed as He was? God viewed their attitude as insubordination, and it angered Him (*see* Numbers 12:1-9). When you resist God's appointed authority, you may find yourself also resisting God, which is a very dangerous place to be.

Disobedience angers the Lord. The prophet Balaam had heard clearly what God told him, but he refused to obey God. His heart was drawn away from God and toward the material profit he could earn. This angered the Lord (*see* Numbers 22:9-22).

Discouraging others kindles God's anger. When the ten spies came back from the Promised Land and gave the people of Israel an evil report, they discouraged them with their negative, fearful reports. This greatly angered the Lord (*see* Numbers 32:10-13).

Disrespectful attitudes toward the Lord infuriate Him. When Moses struck the rock in anger twice instead of speaking to the rock to yield water, his actions so angered the Lord that it kept Moses from entering into the land of promise (*see* Numbers 20:1-12; Psalm 106:32). Disrespectful attitudes toward God can be very costly.

Backsliding also angers God. The Lord had greatly blessed King Solomon with unprecedented wisdom, riches, and fame, yet he turned his heart away from the Lord (*see* 1 Kings 11:4-9; Deuteronomy 6:16; 7:4; 11:16,17; 29:24-28; 32:15-22). When God has done great things in our lives and we turn away from Him, it angers Him.

Stealing the tithe is taking what rightfully belongs to the Lord, and this angers Him. The story of Achan's trespass in Joshua 7 is a prime example. The Lord doesn't ask for much, and when we are unwilling to give the small amount He requests to prove our love for Him, it angers Him. The entire book of Malachi talks about this.

Misrepresenting God ignites His anger. When Job's friends said wrong things about the Lord and misrepresented His character, it angered Him (*see* Job 42:7).

Wickedness kindles the Lord's anger. David wrote in Psalm 7:11 that "… God is angry with the wicked every day."

Nations that treat Israel wrongly greatly anger the Lord. Egypt's enslavement of God's people is a good example. Psalm 78:49 says, "He cast upon them the fierceness of his anger, wrath, and indignation, and trouble…."

It is important to know what angers God so you can stay away from those things.

Other Important Facts About God's Anger

Thankfully, God is *slow to anger*. Again and again, the Bible says things about God, such as, "… [He is] ready to pardon, gracious and merciful, slow to anger, and of great kindness…" (Nehemiah 9:17). Similar statements are found in Psalm 103:8; Joel 2:13; Jonah 4:2; and Nahum 1:3.

When God does get angry, His anger endures but for a moment (*see* Psalm 30:5). Once a person repents of his or her trespass, He turns aside His anger (*see* Psalm 78:38), and His anger ceases (*see* Psalm 85:4). In fact, Psalm 103:9 declares, "He will not always chide: neither will he keep his anger for ever." God delights in mercy and therefore chooses not to be angry toward those who repent.

If you have disobeyed God's instruction — it you have trespassed or violated something He has told you to do or not to do — repent, get back on track, and begin moving forward again. If you have acted like Achan and taken the Lord's firstfruits, or things that belong to Him, ask Him to forgive you and begin taking the necessary steps to make things right. Instead of suffering the consequences of disobedience, repent quickly and receive God's mercy. He is for you, not against you, and His anger will not last forever.

STUDY QUESTIONS

**Study to shew thyself approved unto God, a workman that needeth
not to be ashamed, rightly dividing the word of truth.
— 2 Timothy 2:15**

1. In your own words, briefly describe the difference between *sin* and *a trespass*.
2. How would you define an "accursed thing" as described in this lesson?
3. Carefully read Romans 5:12-19 and identify *the consequences of disobedience* we all received through Adam's actions, as well as *the fruit of obedience* we received through Jesus' actions. (Also *consider* 1 Corinthians 15:21,22,45-49.)

PRACTICAL APPLICATION

**But be ye doers of the word, and not hearers only,
deceiving your own selves.
—James 1:22**

1. Of all the things that kindle the anger of God, which have you struggled with most?

2. Rick shared about not having a full revelation on tithing many years ago when he was first married and how that violation produced lack in his life. Be honest: Do you struggle with giving the Lord His tithe? If so, why? (If you don't know, pray and ask the Holy Spirit to show you what's going on in your heart.) What has happened in your life as a result of your struggle to give Him what is rightfully His?

3. If you have disobeyed God in any area, take time now to repent and ask Him to forgive you. Begin taking the necessary steps to make things right; get back on track and begin moving forward again.

LESSON 4

TOPIC

Getting Back on Track to Victory

SCRIPTURES

1. **Joshua 7:1-12** — But the children of Israel committed a trespass in the accursed thing: for Achan, the son of Carmi, the son of Zabdi, the son of Zerah, of the tribe of Judah, took of the accursed thing: and the anger of the Lord was kindled against the children of Israel. And Joshua sent men from Jericho to Ai, which is beside Beth-haven, on the east side of Bethel, and spake unto them, saying, Go up and view the country. And the men went up and viewed Ai. And they returned to Joshua, and said unto him, Let not all the people go up; but let about two or three thousand men go up and smite Ai; and make not all the people to labour thither; for they are but few. So there went up thither of the people about three thousand men: and they fled before the men of Ai. And the men of Ai smote of them about thirty and six men: for they chased them from before the gate even unto Shebarim,

and smote them in the going down: wherefore the hearts of the people melted, and became as water. And Joshua rent his clothes, and fell to the earth upon his face before the ark of the Lord until the eventide, he and the elders of Israel, and put dust upon their heads. And Joshua said, Alas, O Lord God, wherefore hast thou at all brought this people over Jordan, to deliver us into the hand of the Amorites, to destroy us? would to God we had been content, and dwelt on the other side Jordan! O Lord, what shall I say, when Israel turneth their backs before their enemies! For the Canaanites and all the inhabitants of the land shall hear of it, and shall environ us round, and cut off our name from the earth: and what wilt thou do unto thy great name? And the Lord said unto Joshua, Get thee up; wherefore liest thou thus upon thy face? Israel hath sinned, and they have also transgressed my covenant which I commanded them: for they have even taken of the accursed thing, and have also stolen, and dissembled also, and they have put it even among their own stuff. Therefore the children of Israel could not stand before their enemies, but turned their backs before their enemies, because they were accursed: neither will I be with you any more, except ye destroy the accursed from among you.

2. **1 John 1:9** — If we confess our sins, he is faithful and just to forgive us our sins, and to cleanse us from all unrighteousness.

SYNOPSIS

Jericho was a place of great victory for the people of Israel. It was the first city in the land of promise to fall at their hands. Its destruction put fear into the hearts of the nations throughout Canaan. God's people had heard His instructions and followed them explicitly.

Yet in the process of taking the city, Israel committed a trespass — they knowingly violated God's instructions. Actually, it was only *one man*, Achan, who committed the trespass. Being the first city to be captured, Jericho and all its spoils were consecrated to God. It was the firstfruits of all the land the Lord was giving to Israel. But Achan had secretly taken of the "accursed thing," and the anger of the Lord was kindled against the entire nation as a result (*see* Joshua 7:1). Achan's disobedience opened the door for Israel to be defeated at Ai.

The emphasis of this lesson:

If we disobey God and open the door for trouble to enter our lives, we need to repent and take the necessary steps to get back on track to victory.

Failing To Seek God Before Taking Action Often Proves Disastrous

Not long after Israel's mighty victory over Jericho, the Bible says, "… Joshua sent men from Jericho to Ai, which is beside Beth-aven, on the east side of Beth-el, and spake unto them, saying, Go up and view the country. And the men went up and viewed Ai" (Joshua 7:2). With a major win under his belt, Joshua and his men were feeling confident. Even though he had received no apparent orders from God to attack Ai, he seemed anxious to take it. Thus, without Heaven's instructions, he began making plans.

The city of Ai was small, so the spies Joshua sent out "assumed" it would be easily taken down — especially after the supernatural victory they had experienced at Jericho. Joshua 7:3 says, "And they returned to Joshua, and said unto him, Let not all the people go up; but let about two or three thousand men go up and smite Ai; and make not all the people to labour thither; for they are but few."

Notice whom Joshua was listening to: his spies, not the Spirit of the Lord. This was a major mistake. He leaned on the wisdom of men and as a result acted presumptuously. Verse 4 says, "So there went up thither of the people about three thousand men: and they fled before the men of Ai." The word "fled" indicates that the men of Israel *fled in terror*.

The Bible says, "…The men of Ai smote of them about thirty and six men: for they chased them from before the gate even unto Shebarim, and smote them in the going down: wherefore the hearts of the people melted, and became as water" (Joshua 7:5). The word for "smote" used here implies that these 36 men were *massacred*. This was the first time Israel had lost any men after crossing the Jordan River.

You may wonder, *How could such a small army terrorize 3,000 men of Israel, chase them down, and slaughter some of them?* The reason is that Joshua acted without consulting the will of God. Although it is wisdom to seek godly advice from others, ultimately you need to hear and heed what God is saying. After suffering this defeat, Israel sank in their hearts and melted in fear. They were broken, embarrassed, and humiliated — especially after having just experienced an amazing victory over Jericho.

Joshua and the Elders Earnestly Sought God

Joshua was totally undone. The Bible says he "...rent his clothes, and fell to the earth upon his face before the ark of the Lord until the eventide, he and the elders of Israel, and put dust upon their heads" (Joshua 7:6).

This verse gives us five important things to which we need to pay attention.

First, it says, Joshua "rent his clothes." In Scripture, this represents *sorrow* and means Joshua was *repentant*. His actions were not just a dramatic presentation. He was truly sorrowful before the Lord that he had acted presumptuously and had suffered loss.

Second, Joshua "fell to the earth on his face." This signifies *humility*; he was truly broken before the Lord.

Third, the Bible says, he "fell before the Ark of the Lord." This means *he bowed himself in God's presence*. Joshua was truly seeking God.

Fourth, it says Joshua was doing this with his leaders "until eventide." This lets us know he didn't rush into God's presence and then rush out. *He and his leaders humbled themselves for a prolonged period of time and seriously repented for their actions.* They earnestly sought the face of God and took an inventory of themselves. When you seriously seek the face of God to know the reasons for your defeat, He will answer you and show you just as He did for Joshua.

Fifth, the Bible says Joshua and the elders "put dust on their heads." This was *a symbol of genuine repentance*. They were sincerely penitent in the presence of the Lord.

Joshua Voiced His Frustration

At that point, "Joshua said, Alas, O Lord God, wherefore hast thou at all brought this people over Jordan, to deliver us into the hand of the Amorites, to destroy us? would to God we had been content, and dwelt on the other side Jordan!" (Joshua 7:7.)

A closer look at what Joshua said here reveals that there was really no truth in it. He would have never been content to live in the wilderness on the other side of the Jordan. This discourse was merely his speaking out of his emotions. Joshua was confused and overwhelmed. Although God had given them victory over Jericho, they had suffered a terrible defeat at Ai, and he couldn't understand why.

He continued: "O Lord, what shall I say, when Israel turneth their backs before their enemies! For the Canaanites and all the inhabitants of the land shall hear of it, and shall environ us round, and cut off our name from the earth: and what wilt thou do unto thy great name?" (Joshua 7:8,9).

The Lord Responded

In desperation, Joshua turned the focus off Israel and on the Lord and His reputation. But God was not worried about His reputation. Having reached His fill of Joshua's words, He said, "…Get thee up; wherefore liest thou thus upon thy face?" (Joshua 7:10.) In other words, God said, "Enough! Get up off the ground." Joshua and the elders had repented, the Lord accepted it, and it was now time to move on.

Once repentance is made, God accepts it, and there is no need to continue to wallow in emotional drama. It only prolongs the pain. Repentance for wrongdoing is required, of course, but getting stuck in regret has no benefit whatsoever. If you have repented of your sin, you need to get up and get back to doing what God has called you to do. That was what He was telling Joshua in this passage.

The Lord continued speaking in verse 11, saying, "Israel hath sinned, and they have also transgressed my covenant which I commanded them: for they have even taken of the accursed thing, and have also stolen, and dissembled also, and they have put it even among their own stuff."

This verse reveals four things Israel did that caused them to be defeated by the people of Ai:

1. **They "transgressed" God's instruction.** Achan was the one who transgressed God's commandment by taking of the "accursed thing," which he knew he wasn't supposed to do, and it affected the whole nation.
2. **They "stole."** Achan took what belonged to God — the firstfruits of His promised inheritance to them.

3. **They "dissembled."** This means Achan *lied* about what he had done.
4. **They "put what they stole among their own stuff."** Achan hid the stolen goods.

Transgressing God's instructions, stealing from Him, lying about your sin, and hiding what you've stolen or what you've done will never produce anything positive. If you do something wrong, you need to be honest and come clean with God. Don't lie or try to hide it. Repent for what you've done and take the needed steps to make things right. Once He forgives you and restores you, get back on the road to victory.

Sin Renders You Defenseless Against Your Enemies

After God pointed out what Israel had done wrong, He said, "Therefore the children of Israel could not stand before their enemies, but turned their backs before their enemies, because they were accursed: neither will I be with you any more, except ye destroy the accursed from among you" (Joshua 7:12).

In His mercy, God pinpointed Israel's problem, revealing it to Joshua when he sought Him in prayer and repented. The reason they couldn't fight and defeat their enemies was because of the hidden sin of Achan. And until that sin was addressed, the Lord's presence would no longer be with Joshua and the people of Israel.

Sadly, many people today are living in sin, totally violating the commandments of God's Word. At the same time, they are asking Him to bless their lives, but it just doesn't work that way. If you have transgressed the commandments of the Lord, knowingly violating what He has said in His Word, you cannot expect to receive His blessings. When you deliberately sin and don't repent, God's shield of defense over your life is removed.

Realize that failure and living defeated are never God's will for you. If you have experienced defeat, you need to stop and take an honest inventory of your life. More than likely, your defeat is a result of something you did wrong along the way. Maybe you acted presumptuously or only listened to the advice of others rather than seeking the Lord's will and direction. Maybe you disobeyed what He told you to do and then lied about it or tried to cover it up. Whatever the case may be, it's time to be honest and come clean with God.

Confession Is Your Best Course of Action

One of the greatest verses found in Scripture is First John 1:9. It says, "If we confess our sins, he is faithful and just to forgive us our sins, and to cleanse us form all unrighteousness." The phrase "if we confess our sins" in Greek actually means *if we agree with God*. In other words, if we will be honest and quit hiding what we did wrong and call the sin or trespass what God calls it, He will be faithful and just to forgive us and cleanse us.

The word "forgive" is the Greek word *aphemi*, which means *to release; to send away; to permanently discharge and never bring it up again*. That is exactly what God does to your sin when you confess it to Him. He permanently releases you from the offense and sends it away forever.

In addition to forgiving you, God also promises to "cleanse" you. The word "cleanse" in Greek means *to totally cleanse*. This is not just an exterior cleansing, but the deepest kind of cleansing possible. This purification that God performs in you is so intense, it is as if you never sinned. This is the kind of work He wants to do in your life. He's just waiting for you to confess.

Friend, it's time to get in His presence and sincerely say, "Lord, please show me why I have suffered defeat." As you listen, the Holy Spirit will reveal the truth about what is going on in your life. If you have sinned, *confess* it — agree with God and call the sin what He calls it. Ask Him to *forgive* you, and He will. He will *cleanse* you so deeply, it will be as if you never sinned.

Then get up and get moving! If you're still breathing, there is more territory for you to take. God has great plans for your life, so get back on track to the victory that awaits you!

STUDY QUESTIONS

Study to shew thyself approved unto God, a workman that needeth not to be ashamed, rightly dividing the word of truth.
— 2 Timothy 2:15

1. Sin will sap you of spiritual strength and render you powerless against the enemy. Yet when you confess your sin to God, He promises to forgive you — *permanently releasing you from the offense* — and He never brings it up again. Take a few moments to meditate on Psalm

103:12; Isaiah 43:25; 44:22; and Micah 7:18. How do these promises encourage you to come clean with God?

2. The apostle Paul understood our need for total dependence on God and declared, "Not because we think we can do anything of lasting value by ourselves. Our only power and success comes from God" (2 Corinthians 3:5 *TLB*). Are you depending on God or yourself to bring victory in your life? (Consider Romans 7:18; John 6:63; 15:5; Zechariah 4:6.)

PRACTICAL APPLICATION

> But be ye doers of the word, and not hearers only,
> deceiving your own selves.
> —James 1:22

1. A major mistake Joshua made was that he listened to his spies instead of seeking the Spirit of God for direction. Stop and think: *Who am I listening to regarding the decisions before me? Is it others, myself, or the Holy Spirit? Who has the final word in my life?*

2. Are you living in defeat, unable to overcome the enemy in your life? Get in God's presence and pray: "Lord, please show me why I have suffered defeat." Then be sill and listen. What is the Holy Spirit showing you?

3. If you have sinned, your best course of action is to *confess* it — agree with God and call the sin what He calls it. Ask Him to *forgive* you, and He will. He will *cleanse* you so deeply, it will be as if you never sinned. After you pray, take a few moments to thank Him for His mercy and loving kindness.

LESSON 5

TOPIC

The Fruit of Obedience

SCRIPTURES

1. **Joshua 7:1** — But the children of Israel committed a trespass in the accursed thing: for Achan, the son of Carmi, the son of Zabdi, the son

of Zerah, of the tribe of Judah, took of the accursed thing: and the anger of the Lord was kindled against the children of Israel.

2. **Joshua 7:6** — And Joshua rent his clothes, and fell to the earth upon his face before the ark of the Lord until the eventide, he and the elders of Israel, and put dust upon their heads.

3. **Joshua 7:10-25** — And the Lord said unto Joshua, Get thee up; wherefore liest thou thus upon thy face? Israel hath sinned, and they have also transgressed my covenant which I commanded them: for they have even taken of the accursed thing, and have also stolen, and dissembled also, and they have put it even among their own stuff. Therefore the children of Israel could not stand before their enemies, but turned their backs before their enemies, because they were accursed: neither will I be with you any more, except ye destroy the accursed from among you. Up, sanctify the people, and say, Sanctify yourselves against to morrow: for thus saith the Lord God of Israel, There is an accursed thing in the midst of thee, O Israel: thou canst not stand before thine enemies, until ye take away the accursed thing from among you. In the morning therefore ye shall be brought according to your tribes: and it shall be, that the tribe which the Lord taketh shall come according to the families thereof; and the family which the Lord shall take shall come by households; and the household which the Lord shall take shall come man by man. And it shall be, that he that is taken with the accursed thing shall be burnt with fire, he and all that he hath: because he hath transgressed the covenant of the Lord, and because he hath wrought folly in Israel. So Joshua rose up early in the morning, and brought Israel by their tribes; and the tribe of Judah was taken. And he brought the family of Judah; and he took the family of the Zarhites: and he brought the family of the Zarhites man by man; and Zabdi was taken. And he brought his household man by man; and Achan, the son of Carmi, the son of Zabdi, the son of Zerah, of the tribe of Judah, was taken. And Joshua said unto Achan, My son, give, I pray thee, glory to the Lord God of Israel, and make confession unto him; and tell me now what thou hast done; hide it not from me. And Achan answered Joshua, and said, Indeed I have sinned against the Lord God of Israel, and thus and thus have I done. When I saw among the spoils a goodly Babylonish garment, and two hundred shekels of silver, and a wedge of gold of fifty shekels weight, then I coveted them, and took them; and, behold, they are hid in the earth in the midst of my tent, and the silver

under it. So Joshua sent messengers, and they ran unto the tent; and, behold, it was hid in his tent, and the silver under it. And they took them out of the midst of the tent, and brought them unto Joshua, and unto all the children of Israel, and laid them out before the Lord. And Joshua, and all Israel with him, took Achan the son of Zerah, and the silver, and the garment, and the wedge of gold, and his sons, and his daughters, and his oxen, and his asses, and his sheep, and his tent, and all that he had: and they brought them unto the valley of Achor. And Joshua said, Why hast thou troubled us? the Lord shall trouble thee this day. And all Israel stoned him with stones, and burned them with fire, after they had stoned them with stones.

4. **Joshua 8:1-3** — And the Lord said unto Joshua, Fear not, neither be thou dismayed: take all the people of war with thee, and arise, go up to Ai: see, I have given into thy hand the king of Ai, and his people, and his city, and his land And thou shalt do to Ai and her king as thou didst unto Jericho and her king: only the spoil thereof, and the cattle thereof, shall ye take for a prey unto yourselves.... So Joshua arose, and all the people of war, to go up against Ai....

SYNOPSIS

When Joshua and the people of Israel attacked Jericho, everyone obeyed God explicitly — except for a man named Achan. Scripture says, "... Achan, the son of Carmi, the son of Zabdi, the son of Zerah, of the tribe of Judah, took of the accursed thing: and the anger of the Lord was kindled against the children of Israel" (Joshua 7:1). This one man's trespass became a curse to the entire nation. Israel's amazing victory over Jericho was dwarfed by their humiliating defeat at Ai. Joshua and the people could go no further until they sought the face of God, repented, and purged themselves of sin.

The emphasis of this lesson:

If you've experienced victory and then fouled things up through disobedience, you don't have to stay in that place of sin and defeat. You can receive God's forgiveness, seek Him, and move forward into victory once again.

Israel Had Sinned and Was Powerless Against Its Enemies

In Joshua 7:1, the Lord said, "The children of Israel committed a trespass in the accursed thing...." We learned in a previous lesson that a "trespass" is not just an ordinary sin. It is *a deliberate violation of God's commandment*. Achan committed a trespass by taking of the "accursed thing," which means he took what rightfully belonged to God.

The Lord had specifically warned Israel not to take any of the possessions of Jericho; they were to be consecrated to the Lord and brought into His treasury (*see* Joshua 6:19). Jericho was the first city in the Promised Land to be captured, and therefore, it was the "firstfruits" that belonged to the Lord. To take anything from Jericho was to take what belonged to God. Achan did this and brought a curse on Israel in that they could no longer stand against their enemies.

The Bible says, "Joshua rent his clothes, and fell to the earth upon his face before the ark of the Lord until the eventide, he and the elders of Israel, and put dust upon their heads" (Joshua 7:6). This is a picture of *genuine repentance*. Joshua and his leaders humbled themselves in God's presence, which is represented by the Ark of the Lord. They then took a personal inventory to learn why failure had occurred.

The Lord Revealed the Trespass

In the midst of Joshua's emotional meltdown, the Lord said to him, "... Get thee up; wherefore liest thou thus upon thy face?" God told Joshua, in effect, "Enough is enough! You've repented and I've forgiven you. It's time to get up and get moving. You can't do anything to rectify what has happened in the past, but you can take action to fix things and move forward into the future.

The Lord then told Joshua, "Israel hath sinned, and they have also transgressed my covenant which I commanded them: for they have even taken of the accursed thing, and have also stolen, and dissembled also, and they have put it even among their own stuff" (Joshua 7:11). God was very clear that someone had deliberately violated His commandment — he had stolen something that belonged to Him, lied about it, and had hidden the goods under his tent.

For that reason, God said, "…The children of Israel could not stand before their enemies, but turned their backs before their enemies, because they were accursed: neither will I be with you any more, except ye destroy the accursed from among you" (Joshua 7:12). As a result of sin in the camp of Israel, they were defeated at Ai, and God vowed His presence would not go with Israel until the sin was eradicated.

God Gave Specific Directions for Exposing and Dealing with the Offender

In answer to the prayers of Joshua and the elders, God gave these specific instructions: "Up, sanctify the people, and say, Sanctify yourselves against to morrow: for thus saith the Lord God of Israel, There is an accursed thing in the midst of thee, O Israel: thou canst not stand before thine enemies, until ye take away the accursed thing from among you" (Joshua 7:13).

Just as God was serious about Israel's dealing with sin, He is serious about your dealing with sin too. Sin opens the door for the enemy to attack you. You cannot stand and be victorious over your enemies if you are participating in known sin. *God wants you to deal with your private issues so they don't lead to public disgrace.*

The Lord went on to tell Joshua, "In the morning therefore ye shall be brought according to your tribes: and it shall be, that the tribe which the Lord taketh shall come according to the families thereof; and the family which the Lord shall take shall come by households; and the household which the Lord shall take shall come man by man. And it shall be, that he that is taken with the accursed thing shall be burnt with fire, he and all that he hath: because he hath transgressed the covenant of the Lord, and because he hath wrought folly in Israel" (Joshua 7:14,15).

This was a very in-depth inventory God was requiring Joshua to take. He was to search "man by man," looking for the perpetrator who trespassed God's commands and took of the "accursed thing." Once found, he was to be destroyed by fire. Fire was the means of purification. Through blatant disobedience, this man had brought "folly" on Israel. The word "folly" signifies *shame, embarrassment, and humiliation* — none of which God wanted for His people.

Joshua Took Immediate Action

Scripture says, "So Joshua rose up early in the morning, and brought Israel by their tribes; and the tribe of Judah was taken: And he brought the family of Judah; and he took the family of the Zar-hites: and he brought the family of the Zar-hites man by man; and Zab-di was taken: And he brought his household man by man; and Achan, the son of Car-mi, the son of Zab-di, the son of Ze-rah, of the tribe of Judah, was taken" (Joshua 7:16-18).

Note that the phrase "man by man" was used three times in five verses, indicating a very thorough investigation. Although it must have been a long, time-consuming process, Joshua was very intentional to root out and deal with the issue of sin. He had a reverential fear of the Lord and took his assignment very seriously, which is an important attitude we should have today.

Once Achan was determined to be the culprit, Joshua said, "...My son, give, I pray thee, glory to the Lord God of Israel, and make confession unto him; and tell me now what thou hast done; hide it not from me..." (Joshua 7:19). Achan answered Joshua, "...Indeed I have sinned against the Lord God of Israel, and thus and thus have I done: When I saw among the spoils a goodly Babylonish garment, and two hundred shekels of silver, and a wedge of gold of fifty shekels weight, then I coveted them, and took them; and, behold, they are hid in the earth in the midst of my tent, and the silver under it" (vv. 20,21).

Achan Admitted His Sin

First, Achan admitted he stole *a Babylonian garment*. This was an extremely expensive and very beautiful piece of clothing. It likely had jewels woven into it and had previously belonged to royalty. This was dedicated to the Lord, but Achan took it for himself. He also took *two hundred shekels of silver* and *a wedge of gold weighing fifty shekels*, which was quite a large sum of money.

Why did Achan commit such a crime? He answered in verse 21 saying, "I coveted them, and took them." Thus, he violated the eighth and tenth Commandments. He *coveted* these accursed items and then *stole* them and *hid* them under his tent. The irony of his thievery is that what he stole, he couldn't even enjoy. He had to keep the items hidden because he knew that what he had done was wrong.

This tells us that *secret sins are not enjoyable.* True, they may be pleasurable for a season (*see* Hebrews 11:25), but they bring much shame, guilt, and condemnation. Achan thought he was gaining something of great value through his actions, but what he gained cost him, his family, and his country terribly.

At first, Achan's conversation with Joshua may look like genuine repentance, but it wasn't. It was simply an *admission of wrong* that he could no longer hide. When a person truly *repents* of wrongdoing, he has a deep sorrow in his heart and a sincere turning toward God for forgiveness. But if Achan had not been caught, he probably would have never confessed to what he'd done.

Israel Came Clean with God and Dealt with Its Sin

After Achan admitted his guilt, "Joshua sent messengers, and they ran unto the tent; and, behold, it was hid in his tent, and the silver under it. And they took them out of the midst of the tent, and brought them unto Joshua, and unto all the children of Israel, and laid them out before the Lord" (Joshua 7:22,23). Interestingly, the Bible says they laid out the stolen goods *before the Lord* — not before Joshua or the people. This signifies that Israel was coming clean with God, hiding nothing from Him.

The Bible says, "Joshua, and all Israel with him, took Achan the son of Zerah, and the silver, and the garment, and the wedge of gold, and his sons, and his daughters, and his oxen, and his asses, and his sheep, and his tent, and all that he had: and they brought them unto the valley of Achor. And Joshua said, Why hast thou troubled us? the Lord shall trouble thee this day. And all Israel stoned him with stones, and burned them with fire, after they had stoned them with stones" (Joshua 7:24,25).

Notice it says they burned "them" with fire. More than likely, Achan's wife and entire family were aware that the "accursed" things were hidden in the tent. They may have even handled them up close. Therefore, in a certain way, they were all guilty in the sight of the Lord and needed to be purged from the nation.

In verse 25, Joshua asked Achan and his family, "Why hast thou *troubled* us?" You need to realize that sin and disobedience always brings trouble. In this case, Achan's trespass caused the loss of 36 men in battle and affected all 36 families. It also produced a loss of confidence and courage in Israel, as well as a loss of time and the loss of victory against Ai. Personally, Achan's sin caused him and his entire family to lose their lives.

The price of disobedience is always much higher than the pleasure it temporarily provides. Sin may seem pleasurable for a season (*see* Hebrews 11:25), but in the end, it always produces loss and death.

Joshua 7:26 says, "And they raised over him a great heap of stones unto this day. So the Lord turned from the fierceness of his anger. Wherefore the name of that place was called, The valley of Achor, unto this day."

Same City, Different Outcome

As soon as the sin was identified and removed, Israel was once again empowered. God restored to them protection, promise, confidence, and victory. "And the Lord said unto Joshua, Fear not, neither be thou dismayed: take all the people of war with thee, and arise, go up to Ai: see, I have given into thy hand the king of Ai, and his people, and his city, and his land: And thou shalt do to Ai and her king as thou didst unto Jericho and her king: only the spoil thereof, and the cattle thereof, shall ye take for a prey unto yourselves..." (Joshua 8:1,2).

Just as God promised total victory over Jericho, He promised total victory with Ai. Only this time He told the people to take and keep all the plunder of the battle for *themselves*. Had Achan only been obedient and patiently waited, he would have had received financial and material blessings far greater than what he had stolen from Jericho.

God was not — and is not — against His people having prosperity; the issue is *priority*. Remember, Jericho was the firstfruits of the new land, and it was God's, not Israel's. The Lord wanted to be honored first — as He still wants to be honored first today.

Joshua 8:3 says, "Joshua arose, and all the people of war, to go up against Ai...." And if you read through the end of the chapter, you'll discover Israel was victorious over Ai. God was with them and God is with you! Don't let sin stop you from defeating your enemies. Confess any sin issue to God, receive His forgiveness, and get back on track to victory!

STUDY QUESTIONS

Study to shew thyself approved unto God, a workman that needeth
not to be ashamed, rightly dividing the word of truth.
— 2 Timothy 2:15

1. God does get angry over sin, but His anger endures but for a moment (*see* Psalm 30:5). According to Psalm 78:38; 85:4; and 103:9, what has God promised to do once you repent of a trespass?

2. In Isaiah 1:19 (*NKJV*), God says, "If you are willing and obedient, you shall eat the good of the land." What fruits of obedience can you identify in Deuteronomy 28:1-14? (Also *consider* Exodus 19:5,6; Deuteronomy 5:29, 33; 1 Kings 3:14; John 15:10; James 1:25.)

PRACTICAL APPLICATION

But be ye doers of the word, and not hearers only,
deceiving your own selves.
— James 1:22

1. The entire nation of Israel was affected by Achan's sin. Has that ever happened to you — has someone else's wrongdoing negatively impacted your life? If so, briefly share what happened.

2. How about your actions? Has sin *in your life* ever negatively impacted an innocent bystander in your life? If so, how?

3. How do Achan's story and your past experiences motivate you to carefully obey God — and if you sin, to deal with it quickly?

A Prayer To Receive Salvation

If you've never received Jesus as your Savior and Lord, now is the time for you to experience the new life Jesus wants to give you! To receive God's gift of salvation that can be obtained through Jesus alone, pray this prayer from your heart:

Jesus, I repent of my sin and receive You as my Savior and Lord. Wash away my sin with Your precious blood and make me completely new. I thank You that my sin is removed, and Satan no longer has any right to lay claim on me. Through Your empowering grace, I faithfully promise that I will serve You as my Lord for the rest of my life.

If you just prayed this prayer of salvation, you are born again! You are a brand-new creation in Christ! Would you please let us know of your decision by going to **renner.org/salvation**? We would love to connect with you and pray for you as you begin your new life in Christ.

Scriptures for further study: John 3:16; John 14:6; Acts 4:12; Ephesians 1:7; Hebrews 10:19,20; 1 Peter 1:18,19; Romans 10:9,10; Colossians 1:13; 2 Corinthians 5:17; Romans 6:4; 1 Peter 1:3

Notes

CLAIM YOUR FREE RESOURCE!

As a way of introducing you further to the teaching ministry of Rick Renner, we would like to send you FREE of charge his teaching, "How To Receive a Miraculous Touch From God" on CD or as an MP3 download.

In His earthly ministry, Jesus commonly healed *all* who were sick of *all* their diseases. In this profound message, learn about the manifold dimensions of Christ's wisdom, goodness, power, and love toward all humanity who came to Him in faith with their needs.

☑ **YES, I want to receive Rick Renner's monthly teaching letter!**

Simply scan the QR code to claim this resource or go to: **renner.org/claim-your-free-offer**

Connect WITH US!

renner.org

facebook.com/rickrenner • facebook.com/rennerdenise

youtube.com/rennerministries • youtube.com/deniserenner

instagram.com/rickrrenner • instagram.com/rennerministries_
instagram.com/rennerdenise